STATE LINES

# STATE LINES

*Poems for the journey home.*

Gold & Light Publishing
*Preston Hornbeck*

To request permission, contact the publisher at
hellostatelines@gmail.com

First Edition Paperback: 978-1-7350813-0-4
eBook Edition: 978-1-7350813-1-1

First paperback edition printed June, 2020

Edited By: Blake Steen
Cover Art: Charlotte Pell & Valina Yen
Cover Design: Valina Yen
Published by: Gold & Light Publishing

goldandlight.co

# A Note from The Author

The best way to create is to first be affected.

The journey of writing this book was filled with moments that affected me. Over the span of six months, I wrote somewhere around 127 poems while traveling across the United States and visiting 10 countries. This book is a curated collection of 61 poems from that time, carefully chosen to tell a story.

In these pages you will find poems of memories that have marked me—moments of beauty and of grief, found within the magnificent and mundane alike.

To share some of the inspiration I found along the way, I've created a QR code to invite you in a little closer.

In downloading a "QR code scanner" app and scanning the code below, you will find photos and videos captured during this adventure, a playlist of songs that inspired me during these travels, and more ways for us to connect.

I offer you my sincerest thanks for reading *State Lines*. I hope your experience with this book is personal, inspiring, and delightful. I'm grateful you're taking this journey with me.

*For*
*Roger Hornbeck*
*1964 - 2019*

# Contents

## Sleep

## State Lines

"Poetry is inclusive, not exclusive. Poetry is humble. It gives up control of saying exactly what we mean, in order to let another find something they need to hear."

— Jessie Miller

## 000 Burned-out

*Dad, I'm 25, and I feel burned out. I have my "dream job," and I don't even want to go to work most mornings.*

Calmly, he posed this question:

*Son, if you could do anything, what would you do?*

His words struck me like lightning. I started listing one disclaimer after another about why I couldn't do what I wanted to do. He waited patiently. Exasperated, I reached my end—

*Dad, if I could do anything, I would write. I would travel the world and write.*

Silence filled the line. Then, with a soft strength he spoke:

*Son, life is short.*

He paused.

*If that is your dream, then go for it.*

## 001 My Voice
Sophia, North Carolina

*Hello*

I said, closing my eyes.
I could see his smile lines.
He was there before me,
nearly a stranger, my old friend.

He spoke and I sighed with relief,
realizing
he had returned to me.

Relief:

like the feeling of coming home to a porch light
on; like curtains dancing in the summer breeze,
through opened windows, to *The Old Favour-*
*ite* song.

With a tone carrying resolve
like the old work barn to the left.
Broken in by outbursts of deep belly laughter
like the trampoline to the right.
Bound to work hard,
equally likely
to steal a squeal of delight.

He stood before me now.
He was there the whole time.

Resting within the shadows
of a strong mountain range.
Shining with hope
is the sound that he brings—

My Voice.

*Following the Light West*

"I went to the woods because I wished to live deliberately, to front only the essential facts of life, and see if I could not learn what it had to teach, and not, when I came to die, discover that I had not lived."

— Henry David Thoreau

## 004 Words from Woods
Sophia, North Carolina

I whisper to the trees.
The trees whisper back to me.

Their crisp, dry leaves rattle with sounds
of pouring rain. Their acorns crash into the tin
roofs around me, a warning of the
thunderstorms to come in spring.

I clearly hear every word they say.

The trees become still in silence. I pause and
take a breath. I too have learned to wait in ten-
sion. I too have learned the art of rest.

Can you hear the words of the woods?
An autumnal tone hints that all things come to
an end. Yet, in a storm of treetops falling,
falls the hope for new life again.

The trees' raining roars
fill the fields of my heart.
They sing,

*You have every reason to hope.*

And these are the words I'll choose to believe
in the winter season
I will soon face at home.

These singing trees have marked me.
Their strong love has held me firm—
teaching me of the tree within,
firmly rooted
in words from woods.

**010 Silence**
Manhattan, New York

I traveled cross country
to her city, down to her very block.

When at the last minute
she chose to stay inside
while I stood
out in the rain.

She did not come downstairs that night.
She did not respond at all.

We never talked.

Horns and sirens yelled at us both—

To me, they urged, "Move on."
To her, they weren't as kind.

Night fell, and I left New York silently
aboard a raging subway train.

The one thing I took away from my trip to
New York City:

What was broken by silence
is not repaired the same way.

**012 Ships**
Toms River, New Jersey

Plopped atop a dock
       at the shipyard by the sea

                when like a ghost in the mist,
                a ship appeared before me.

Still far off in the distance,
walking those trepidus waves
when its foghorn sang its song.

The airy voice cried out:

       *It is time to leave, you who never stay.*

Sea Giant, can you blame me?

Weary ships *know* they cannot stay.

       Foreign harbours will not be homes
       when anchor-hearts are pins
       clinging to the tops of waves.

I must embrace the deep blue.

Passing through
these small port towns
until I find
my place.

### 013 The Warm Current
Seaside, New Jersey

Atlantic, at last we meet—
    how long I've waited
        to taste your salty breeze.

        You are the warm current

However, it is the dead of winter.
It is cold out.

    Still, we've never met before.

    Therefore, I reason,
        I would be insane to refuse
        to swim in you now.

Sweet, sweet rush of life.

**014 Sip**
Smoky Mountains, Tennessee

Sifting through the grains of trees,
heartwarming like ginger tea,
I am water flowing
through the grounds of Tennessee.

Within the grand mountain peaks,
        hidden I sit and steep—
as the arched hills around me
lightly begin to steam.

Then the kettle blows. It is time to go.
The towering billows of fog,
the orange and gold trees burning,
I will not soon forget.

I am grateful to drink in these moments.
Even if only for a sip.

### 015 Following the Light West
Little Rock, Arkansas

Cold hands in the pockets of a hooded coat.
Sailing by frosted lakes.

I travel, following the light back west.

Soft winds blow. Snowflakes fall,
and straight ahead, night still calls.
Silver scene, answer me,
can there be depth in shallow seas?
Frozen ground, be broken down—
we are fire bound.

I swear, our kindle will spark!
My matchbox is full—I will oust the dark.
Do not tell me to retreat now.
My lantern is lit again—I will not burn out.

Around the fire of hope our friendship will
begin. Forgiveness will flicker with orange
flame—
            love will live
and there will be no more blame.

When the moment comes and the sunlight
finally fades,
the fire we have built together
will still guide my way.

Fire, fire, lead me on—carry me with hope.
Fire, fire, lead me on—carry me back home.

## 017 Diet Dr. Pepper
Dallas, Texas

We sit at a table.
Not across from one another—
we sit side by side.

Reminiscing, sweetly;
remembering, slowly.

Sitting eye-to-eye,
savoring
every moment
while we're still able.

Sipping Diet Dr. Pepper,
half in his glass, half in mine.
Speaking softly,
enjoying our slow time.

"I'm not scared of it anymore, you know?"
He says to me. Then continuing,
"I've finally made peace with it...
I've made peace with myself."

Still, neither of us dare say the word—
we dare not mention it.

"You can feel it in your body—
things just start shutting down.
Your body stops working like it used to...
I've felt it for a few years now."

The conversation slows.
There is cancer in his bones.
Sadness has filled our hearts
and our souls cannot bare the weight

so tears trickle out instead of words

as we share
Diet Dr. Pepper
and wait.

We wait for the end
we fear is increasingly near.

We sit together
and wait.

## 018 Father
Dallas, Texas

I go for a walk.
Tears no longer trickle;
now, they rush like a river.

Underneath a streetlight in the dead of night
I vamp my slow building cries.

Jesus comes near.
I feel his presence as I pace.
I cry out my heart.
He hears me
while we wait,
and we talk.

He speaks kindly to me.
He embodies empathy.

And when there are no more words to say,
together, we weep.

He does not take my grief away.
He knows it is what I need.

Together we walk through the dark.
Together we feel the pain.

He tells me he knows
what it is like
to lose a father.

## 020 Blood and Honey
Dallas, Texas

I'm making the drive west again
as a blood and honey sunset
sinks beneath the houses
where beaten hearts rest.

A yellow haze appears in the sun's place:
The remnant of light. Only for a moment—
before daylight is broken by night
and the sky turns back
to dust and grey.

I arrive at dusk
at my father's house.
The soft colors of terminal sunsets.
Blood and bones poisoned,
slowly broken down,
under blood and honey skies
all too quickly fading out.

I see him.
Immediately
our blood pressures climb
like every other time
I've walked into his room
for the last few weeks.

We take in the sunsets.

And as I go he says,

*You don't worry about me!*
*Go and live your life. I'll be fine.*
*If anything starts to get too bad, I'll let you know.*

But will we see each other again eye-to-eye?

Shine.
Shine, you brilliant light of life,
shine underneath these sparkling silver nights.

The radiant glow of a father's smile.
SHINE. SHINE. SHINE.

Oh, strong cheekbones,
hold steady now
under blood and honey skies.

## 025 Blush
Route 66, Arizona

Through the harshest winter conditions
with a hopeful spirit I persist.

Following the power lines
      west,
        I drive.

California is waiting.

Through the desert
I try
to see the beauty of fragile life.

Beautiful Golden Coast,
pull me in close;

can you see I need your help?
Tuck me safely into your soul.

Let your rosy glow
bring the blush back to my cheeks.

Oh, light of the setting west,
pull me in close;
Save me from the aching deep.

### 026 California is on Fire
Redding, California

Brittle copper leaves
       shiver in the chilling breeze
            and their tree bodies
hold their breath

as blankets of ash
fall quickly
and cover the aching floor.

The brave, crippled trees
stand tall
until they can no more.

Barren, the forest becomes
a crematorium overnight.
A wasteland made
of what was once
rich wooded life.

Blackened, condemned,
entire trunks reduced to twigs.

The birds, squirrels, and beavers
flee for their lives
without grabbing their packs,
without saying goodbye. It is time

for us to leave too.

California is on fire again.
       Tell me, if you can,
          where the hell am I supposed to go?

What are we to do?

**028 The Poet Spends New Years Eve by The Ocean**
Los Angeles, California

The horizon of burning orange fades
to a gradient of gold and pink
on New Years Eve
over that great forgiving sea.

The fishermen of the wharf
drop their lines into deep ocean blues.
They cast weighted lures
while I throw something more.
The sea ripples repeatedly.

Coinlike, the pressure
of the year before
falls to the ocean floor to drown.

In the final hours of the last day,
an entire year is washed away—
and my soul is brined by the sea.

And I let myself believe.

## 031 Frost and Warmth
Lake Tahoe, Nevada

Shining snow covered caps are standing tall
over sparkling white blanketed paths.
We set course in one van with ten boots
to explore a frigid winter forest with nothing
else to do.

We sweep the quickly collecting snow off our
clothes. Then we swipe the frost from our
beards and our snow topped toes.

Looking out, the water stands sturdy—a beau-
tiful frozen lake—still, distant streams whisper
gently to us:  An almost silent praise.

The sky mirrors the water's depth, reflecting
the scene: the clearest blues and whites your
eyes have ever seen.

A fox trots by with bushy tail,
and I see that though the winter season is
bitter,
in morning light,
hope throughout all of nature swells.

I fix my eyes upon the mountains.

In this moment—in the silence and stillness—
it has never been more evident
that you, my God, are teaching me resilience.

Therefore, before I feel the warmth of spring,
I choose to hope in you. I choose to see your
goodness. I choose to trust that your promises
remain true.

Before I know how it all works out:

I declare you are faithful.
Though I may fall short,
in you I have no doubt.

Thank you for this season of frost and
uncertainty.

Thank you for the moments
where you are the only thing I can see.

I lean into you fully,
and believe your promises even now,
for in the harshest of winter snows,
you still won't let me down.

## 032 Home
Redding, California

The resistance I feel
is overwhelmingly real.

I find myself dragging my feet,
nearly unable to leave.

Still, I carry on toward the door.

Exchanging my home
for a new song on my tongue—
and the rush of unknown lands.

There is no safety
in being the foreigner.

I will be the foreigner there.
But I have become the foreigner here.

So tell me, which is better?

I know it is time to leave.

40 |

**036 Novo**
Redding, California
*for Lucas dos Santos*

*Hey, play a C.*
*Harmonize with me!*

We both enjoy the in-between—
the space filled with grace—
where we wait
in silence
for the next chord to shape.

Listen—Can you hear the sound
the record player makes
before the vinyl begins?
Scratching as it starts to turn,
right before the first note fades in?

*Emigrate.*

Our story unfolds as something else is taking
place. It's sad, but not tragic—it's simply
another lap around *Round Lake*.

This spin requires me to leave our sacred space.

Before I go, I want to ask you: Do you know
the sound of my favorite melody?

It is the when the two of us
make up songs and intentionally sing off-key.
Then our laughs fill the halls;
and dance over our newly carpeted floors, and
echo off the freshly painted walls.

I'm afraid we have come to the end of that
song. However, I feel in my bones
that this silence will not last long.

Your songs will never die in my mind.
You were an *Anchor* in my life.
And the sound of your life is divine.

Until the next time our tuned instruments
meet, I will *Carry You* with me,
always, in the key of C.

*Borderline*

"Courage, dear heart."

— C.S Lewis

## 039 The First Day of Rain
Rio de Janeiro, Brazil

in a city that only shines.
        The clouds cover every ray of light
            and only I know why.

The rain falls without relenting,
        the trees seem completely unaware;
            people pay the drops no mind,

yet me, I see it all

—every drop, every fall, every time.

## 040 Opened Windows
Rio de Janeiro, Brazil

In the summer breeze,
the night is pleasant as can be.

The wind comes as it wishes,
and leaves the same way.

Let's not be so bold as to think
we have any control
over such delicate things.

## 042 Lights Colliding
Paris, France

Two souls collide
in the City of Love
  like explosions of light,
    lingering fireworks,
      illuminating the dark blue above.

And with her fingers at rest in my hands,
  my heart beats with ease.

For a body that has sailed the skies,
  chasing every shooting star,
  finally, there is no reason to leave.

The searching has become the settled.

How adventurous it is
to love.

**045 When We Met in the Garden**
Garden of Gethsemane, Jerusalem, Israel

We don't deserve this,
this Holy, righteous thing you've done—

*Child, your unworthiness*
*is far outmatched*
*by my love.*

*You deserve what I paid for with blood.*

**047 The Stones of Time**
Milan, Italy

We are the cathedrals, monumentally tall,
standing on cold cobblestoned
Italian streets.

I attempt to pen this magic.

I cannot.

Wonder fills my lungs as words evade my tongue.
Statuelike, I am stilled by beauty.

I conclude that stories shared
will never compare to the breathtaking moments

      that wildhearts bear.

Still, I will go on
writing poems, taking photos, telling stories:
carving my life
into the stones of time.

But now I know
that the memory holders
hold the greatest glories.

**048 Carry You**
Lausanne, Switzerland

Sleepy heads stumbled on
          half asleep.
Shoulder leans—never enough—
          the crutch to my walk.

Then

into the great white mountains:
          we were swallowed by
          endless serenity.

And I'm glad
that in the cold deep,
you were there with me.

**049 Borders**
London, England

You are lost in a forest of language—
a world of words unknown.
Guided by a distant north star,
a faraway shimmer you call "hope."

You live in silence.
   You, the immigrant.
Unable to make a sound.

    *Emigrate. Emigrate. Emigrate,*
    you think.

Your willful heart won't listen.

    *Emigrate. Emigrate. Emigrate,*
    playing on repeat.

You are a long way from home,
but at least you're in a Kingdom.
Is this everything you wanted?
Everything you dreamed of?

You know the coastline isn't far—
you could go back any time.

But no, you will stay.
A fool in pursuit of life, love, and the like—
trapped within the borders of your own dreams.

## 052 Orange and Golden Lights
Madrid, Spain

Exploring
Madrid, Spain,
where lovers walk
    in El Retiro Park.
    We have joined the great parade
        of orange and golden lights burning,
        bursting through great glass houses.
        Oh, how I wish we could stay.
    But into our crystal palace,
    the place where love resides,
jealousy has entered—
our structure's compromised.
We are shattering.

And I'm left holding rocks
with no place
to hide.

**055 Rest**
Oporto, Portugal

I find rest at the family table.

I can breathe easily.
I am finally somewhere
where they know me.

There is no trying to *be* someone.
There is no talk I cannot understand.

Soon, I will travel back to bed
for a nap.

How our minds and bodies
need a day of rest.

Good Lord, help my heart find it too.

## 057 Birdsong (Closed Windows)
Rio de Janeiro, Brazil

All the birds flew away,
so I stopped looking out the window.
I sat on your bed,
crossed my legs,
and wrote this poem.

I flew all this way
looking out an airplane window
so I could sit on your bed,
cross my legs,
and write this poem?

You flew away
out your bedroom window,
gone to sing your birdsong.

I am still here on your bed,
crossing my legs,
writing this poem.

Tomorrow I will be gone.

*Sleep*

"I tell you this
to break your heart,
by which I mean only
that it break open and never close again
to the rest of the world."

— Mary Oliver

**061 When Cities Finally Burn**
Houston, Texas

Someday I hope to set a book on fire.
It might be a poetic injustice—
or the flint that sparks a revolution.
Unabridged, uncondensed,
transforming soldiers to doctors
and strangers to friends.

The burning pages will light lanterns,
those flickering metal street posts
that guide the lost souls home
where they are free to burn.
Where they will always burn.

And after all the wars have finally worn thin,
when it is safe to be a walking torch again,
then you will not find me there in the streets.

I will have returned to where I am from—
beautifully ablaze, consumed by fire,
standing beside the sun.

**064 Spill**
McKinney, Texas

In the dining room,
sitting on top of the mahogany table
is a glass cup that is beginning to spill over.
My hand holds true and steady
while the pitcher continues to pour
and the water flows over the rim
and down the smoothed octagonal angles.

With my fingers dripping wet,
    the pitcher continues to pour,
        and it creates a massive puddle on the table
            that runs like a river to the floor.

        How easy it can be to get carried away,
            how relieving.

## 065 Gold to Gold
Dallas, Texas

It appears that God is dead-set
on me
making it.

I draw this conclusion
from the countless times
I have fallen

only to find myself
moving forward:

From dust to dust
          gold to gold
                    glory to glory.

## 066 Sleep
Dallas, Texas

There on my favorite floral couch
I laced my fingers behind my head.

Reclining back, I stretched out my legs. Ankles
crossed, I kicked my shoes off. My feet barely
reached the armrest. I stared at my blue and
black spotted socks. I wiggled my toes and
shifted my lower back, trying to find the perfect
position to relax.

Growing tired of seeking sleep, I took the first
pillow, turned onto my side, and tucked it
between my knees. The second pillow I made
sure was a firm support for my head—but the
couch was proving no better than the bed. The
third pillow I choked close to my chest.

It is all to no avail. I lay void of rest.

No matter what I try,
the night remains my enemy—
and daily this repeats—

It is impossible to put my thoughts to bed
when my father is approaching sleep.

## 068 Remember
Lewisville, Texas

Arms crossed at the Perc.
Our daily outing—our morning cup of coffee.

My eyes cast down, hands trying
to conceal my face
when you lean in from across the table.

Moved by my need,
you reach out
and lay your hand on my arm.

My walls of pain do not stop you
from drawing near.
You deconstruct my house of loneliness
brick by brick
and my heavy heart
is alleviated.

You wipe away the lie that I am alone.

And your hand squeezes my arm tightly,
a comfort—you won't let go.

Through my tears and despite my unstable
frame, your gentle hand lifts my head.

Cradling my face in your palms, you look me in
the eyes.

With one gaze,
warmth floods my soul.

And I believe you
when you gently say,

> *I am still in control.*

## 071 Death and Feelings
Dallas, Texas

Outside the entrance to admissions,
I determined the box was no longer needed.
I opened it up, removed the ring, and threw the
shell in the dirt. Laid to rest in the flowerpots
of a hospital gift shop, I buried my ring case
and left that coffin to rot.

Then, I pushed the chair into the elevator.

I prepared him to go upstairs.
I placed the ring on my finger
and the cold, cold metal, I could feel.

Petrified upon arrival,
I removed the ring
and placed it back in my pocket—
unable to take the feeling any longer.

I wheeled him into the doctor's office.

The doc read us the bad numbers. Numbly, I
sat and watched him.

There was still a fire inside my father's eyes
when the tears came streaming out.

*I'm not ready to give up yet, what do we try now?*

God damn a hopeless narrative!
There has to be more than their steroids and
bullshit sedatives.

Leaving the office, I could feel a black hole in
my stomach begin to swirl.

Nauseated, I wanted to cry.

Then, I remembered the bird I saw earlier that
morning—
the one outside the glass window downstairs—
the one that hit the window and died.

I pushed the chair back into the elevator.

I prepared my father to go upstairs.
I placed the ring back on my finger
and the cold, cold metal, I could feel.

## 074 Teammates and Blue Delphiniums
Dallas, Texas
*When Brent, Hobie, & Conrad flew to town for*
*Dad's Memorial Service*

You and I grew up together.
And you and I will sit together
at the end of the day,
telling stories on the steps
of the front porches we have not yet built.

Day by day, we'll go on
building our homes together.
Our 21 year history is only a foreshadowing.

Through time and tide,
you've been by my side.
You were there
when I needed you most.

You are a good friend.
How could I ever thank you for that?

All day until dark,
and through dark until the light—

I'm convinced
we will always be teammates.

## 076 Wonder
Flower Mound, Texas

I walked the salt flats of the vast American
Southwest, where earth and heaven connect in
purple sunsets.

I rode my bike with a headwind behind me
through midwestern plains.

I climbed mountains, red rocks, and boulders,
grateful for each foothold of awe.

I wandered beneath great green chandeliers
hanging hundreds of feet above:
the Redwoods.

I ventured  into deep ocean homes;
crystal shingled roofs, rainbow floored reefs.

I stood silent in chilled air
filled with wonder by snow-covered Swiss Alps.

+

Still,
in every place
the story was inescapably the same.

Each place my foot has tread,
I have yet to experience
a lack of You.

: You are everywhere.

## 078 My Friend, Paul
McKinney, Texas
*For Paul Frey*

Under a mountain hat
sat the man named Paul.
Across from a friend drinking a cap,
drawing his friend named Paul.

Yesterday Paul was ill.
Today he feels much better.
Last week Paul drove from California to Texas,
through a blizzard.

Don't talk to *us* about bad weather.

Paul knew his friend felt scared and alone.
So Paul drove 30 hours
to play games and tell stupid jokes.

Many times,
Paul and his friend
have enjoyed talking about deep things—
matters of life-and-death, neuropsychology,
and being spiritual beings.

But this week,

this week is a week
for deep talks *and* stupid jokes.

How nice it is
that Paul and his friend
are the kind of friends
that can do both.

## 085 Bodies of Glass
Broken Arrow, Oklahoma

Bless those brave souls
who make their hearts a lake
where we may
explore and express, bathe and breathe
in what they create.

Long live the artists,
the ones that pour their souls
into fresh bodies of emotion
and let melodies flow.

Thank you, you beautiful givers,
you who live as bodies of glass,
you who put your hearts on display.

You give depth to today.

I pray you never stop making waves.

## 086 Oil
Flower Mound, Texas

Settle down, you're broken down,
you whose oil has run out.

It dripped and dropped
until all was lost—
black gold on the ground.

Settle down, you've sputtered out,
your slow leak became a bleed.

It all passed fast.
Oil doesn't last. There's no driving
away from this street.

There's so much more I want to say.
But now it's too late to speak.

I'll live with you forever
in my memory,
still alive
in every breath I breathe.

Settle down. Settle down. Settle down.

You cannot pick up the drops
that have already fallen out.

There's no more idling
or turning over now.

But one day we'll drive
the backroads together again.

**090 Decomposing**
Flower Mound, Texas

I am waiting within a winter field
that was once full
of blooming wildflowers.

They may return with Spring's arrival.

The lost and decomposing have been buried.
The soil is rich and abundant.
Death has become the potent fertilizer.

I pray the rain returns in April or May.
The flowers too
will then return to smile at the sky.

But April or May
is not today.

This field is a winter field
filled with the promise
of beauty in spring—but today,
the stench of loss is still overwhelming,
and spring is not today.

*State Lines*

You can never go home again, but the truth is you can never leave home, so it's all right.

– Maya Angelou

## 093 We Were the Sunflowers
Hesston, Kansas

We were the seeds that came from hundreds of
miles away.

Planted in the earth behind the wheat fields,
we sprouted up into the windy plains.

Then sheltered by the smiles of those
who welcomed us in warmly
to fields they called home.
For a couple of glorious years,
we too called those fields home.

We became buds there, rooted in the dirt and
mud there; we took those fields with no names
and made them our place of fame.

Bless the souls that watered us—
those that made space and guarded us,
who never ceased to offer
the love and safety we needed to bloom.

There, we were given the proper conditions
and taught to tear down our fences.

We learned to seek the sun in each season.

From seeds to buds, then buds to proud stocks
we grew
in the overlooked, marvelous midwestern
plains.

We were the sunflowers.
Perpetually opened to the sun.
Prepared to start there
and go everywhere.

## 096 Artists in the Mountains
Morrison, Colorado

Two men meet—wanderers of the Rocky
Mountains.

They have come to the red rocks
seeking solitude.
They have not found it—

they have found each other.

Strangers,
unexpected gifts walking strange places.

A painter, near 70 and retired.
A poet, 26, appearing equally as tired.

United by their arts.
Cowboys turned companions.
Trailblazers, taming their wild hearts.

Strangers,
unexpected gifts walking strange places.

When they leave,
two friends part.

## 099 State Lines
Moab, Utah

I see your
mountain tops, red canyon lands,
muddy rivers, hot desert sands.

> Sleeping in my Jeep by night, pressing
> onwards by day.
> Until I finally feel that *home*
> is a place that I can stay.

A rush for adventure led me out
and developed into a lifestyle of discomfort.

I guess I'm still doubting
what I've been given—and don't feel I deserve.

> This is what it looks like when a man
> second-guesses his worth.

I roll on

through the cracks of my country.

My vocal cords pressed and stretched.
Pressure building on my back and neck.

I wish there had been a forewarning—
or an aiding clairvoyance—
that I would get more than I bargained for
isolated en voyage.

I am headed home.

> Now, more than ever I see,
> endless state lines
> are no comparison
> to *your* company.

## 100 Wilderness
Fallon, Nevada

Driving 100 miles per hour
10,000 thoughts per minute
down the loneliest highway in America.

I swear this time I'm in it.

Abandoned houses with roofs ripped open
wilting dozens of miles apart—
keepers of the desert:
empty and falling apart.

I soar past them all,
with bone-dry mountain walls on both sides;
one still hiding the remnants of snow in its
shadow,
the other bare, stripped, and exposed by the
light.

I soar past the deserted, the lonely, the bare—
slowly making progress from the depths of hell
through the middle of nowhere.

And in the wilderness, this is the one thing I've
learned:

though the heart be not void of hope,
progress is not void of hurt.

## 101 Chasing the Light
Redding, California
*For Noah Baker*

*I'm home!*

I exclaim.
You shut the door behind me.
I have returned from life on the road.

*It's so good to see you!* You say.
*Welcome home, friend. Can you stay a while?*
*When do you depart?*

*I'm not sure yet. Maybe a week or two,* I say.

We smile disappointed smiles.

*You've come a long way,* you say.
*I can see it in your eyes!*

I drop my bag by the door
and walk into the room with high ceilings.
We sit down for a meal,
like so many times before.

And as I leave, you say,

*Press on, keep chasing the light.*

### 102 Old Green Car
Redding, California

The end of a chapter.
I sold that old green car.
A decade of escapades and suspense spent in
the driver's seat.

Cross country, my country
was found behind that steering wheel.
Home within four doors.
Windows down, radio blaring—I'm sure they
always will be.

There is no rest for us old bulls.
Our tanks perpetually half full,
running toward setting suns.

This next road I walk alone.

Old Green Car,
You were safe when life was not.
To most, an old green car—to me, a shelter.

*Eastern Twilight*

If you know you're going home, the journey is never too hard.

– Angela Wood

## 103 Red-eye
Manila, Philippines

*I don't know where to go from here.*

Matt from Relient K tells me not to blink.
And I respect his opinion
so I'll listen to his advice
regardless of what my other friends think.

Matt, should I listen to them?
Or should I listen to my heart?
I thought I could trust both.

Matt says opinions fade like wind,
but hearts are permanent.

I sit and listen for more—

*Love is beautiful and true, life is beautiful and new.*

This is a moment.

So rather than dipping my toes in the water,
I will dive straight in, per usual.

To live life as my true self, I have died.

These are the happenings of a red-eye flight.
And with every horizon I fly into,
I am waking up to life.

**105 Disneyland**
Tokyo, Japan

Today it rained
at the happiest place on earth.
We'll look for something else.
Pray this still works,
but right now it's raining
and rain can't reverse.

## 107 Ultralight Aviation
Tsukuba, Japan

Dear Friend,

I will be an open field for you.

You don't have to fly any farther alone—
let your guard and landing gear down.

Though I am only one field in your flightpath,
I will always be a safe place to land.

Land.

### 108 Cream and Sugar
Tsukuba, Japan

Please don't punish me now—
I'm busy beating myself up,
burning my tongue daily
with the coffee in this cup.

I come back for more,
hoping my wrongs will be poured out
and the pressure blown away like steam.
Can you believe this?
Can you blame me?

I swear I thought
this was helping.
In hindsight, I feel silly.

Will you save me now
from burning with my coffee?

It's too bitter.

You and you alone
are sweet like sugar
and smooth like cream.

## 110 Cherry Blossom
Unknown Mountainside, Japan

There's still one last cherry blossom tree
full bloom in the Japanese countryside.
There's still one last cherry blossom tree—
the others have wilted and died.

On top of this mountain
I realize
these out-of-season fireworks
are all I need—
beauty.

And as I leave at tomorrow's daybreak—
if all I have is this last cherry blossom tree,
I can wait contently
until next spring.

## 111 Ghost
Ota, Gunman, Japan

I have traveled more in six months
than most do in a lifetime.
I am not bragging.

By now, it's gotten harder and harder
to believe the lie
that traveling is what I want.

I have freely explored
with thousands of people in hundreds of places.
In every place,
I've felt a little more lost,
a little more alone.

I'm dying to feel at home.

I've lived the life I always wanted.
40 more hours a week
for the canyons, shores, and mountain peaks.
And at the end,
my heart still feels haunted.

This ghost has followed me for years.
The ghost that convinces me to run.
"There's always somewhere else—"

I'm done.

## 112 In the Passenger Seat,
Tatebayashi-sho, Japan

I am feeling sad.
I still miss my dad.

## 114 Hair
Nagoya, Japan

When my father died
I let my hair grow long.

When your mind is broken
it does strange things
to help you move along.

My father knew those hairs
so I refused to cut them off.
Undesirable was the growth
that time would not put off.

My hair grew longer and longer
but my father stayed gone—
so I cried into the mirror
and cut my hair in shame
but my father was still gone.

The hair I have now
has never been known
by his hands.

He has never run his fingers
through these confused locks
and gently told me it'll all be okay
and that he understands.

Now, my hair has grown long again
and the pain is there still.

Until the day
the slow inching forward fades,
I'm not sure the pain will split or end—
I don't think it ever will—
I don't think it can.

*The Journey Home*

"I still don't know how to work out a poem,"
she said.

"A poem needs understanding through the
senses. The point of diving in a lake, is not im-
mediately to swim to the shore, but to be in the
lake; to luxuriate in the sensation of water. You
do not work the lake out, it is an experience be-
yond thought. Poetry soothes and emboldens
the soul to accept mystery."

— John Keats, *Bright Star*

**118 Drop**
Redding, California

This cloud has never felt like home.
Though I've tried to stay
compatible with comfortable,
the draw to be rainfall
is much too strong.

My vapor condensed
appears different from the makeup
of other raindrops,
and I can't help but feel
that I was uniquely made for this.

No other drop of rain
could live this fall.

This is my moment.
I creep to the thundering grey ledge—
and let go of it.

Descending from the sky,
I am terrified.
I try to stop someway, somehow,
but I am flying full force toward the bottom.

And right when I think
there's no way I could take the impact—SPLASH!

I land into the careful hands of the Ocean
and I find myself more at home than I've ever
felt before.

All it took
was all of me falling.
Nothing less, nothing more.

## 119 Mr. Pine
Redding, California

Mr. Pine, tell me, do you mind getting so wet?
The rain is cold and there's nothing you can
do—your branches look heavy,
and you look like you're crying, too!

Mr. Man, I am not so scared of the rain.
It is here now, but it always goes away.
My roots sure do like it, it makes them much
stronger—but if I may be so bold, Mr. Man,
by the droop of your branches,
I'd say that you can't take it much longer.

That's right, Mr. Pine, it bothers me something
fierce! I am drenched, exhausted, and past the
point of tears. You see, I am standing where I
was told, but I was not made to endure all of
this cold.

I see, Mr. Man. That seems like much to bear.
Let me ask you, friend, do you trust the man
that planted you there? Do you know better
than he how much rain you can withstand?
Or are you both the growing and the maker
of your land? If what you have tried has not
worked thus far, then why not try what I do?

And what is it exactly that you do, Mr. Pine?
Tell me plainly, what are you proposing that I
try?

Mr. Man, let the wind lift your head to the sky.
Hold out your branches and let the rain wash
you clean. This rain will end, just as all rain
does, but trust that the rain is important
to all of your being.

**121 Iced Latte**
Redding, California

There's a sweet drink in my hand and a bitter
taste left in my mouth.
One last coffee from my favorite spot
before I drive south.

I've said my goodbyes.
I've sold my things.

The highway signs will say this is right—
I question them but continue;
when your heart is lost,
nearly any route forward will do.

This is no different than before—
this is what I know.
A million sad farewells
is the toll of life on the road.

## 122 Abraham
Los Angeles, California

*It is time to set course for a new land.*
*Go from your country and your kindred. Leave*
*your father's house and everything in it.*
*I will be with you.*

Held safely within the seed of unaware men,
still bearing the fruit of germination,
the promise to the ancient father
carries on from
generation to
generation.

*It is time to set course for a new land.*

I'll count all as lost and follow you there.

Above every promise or possibility,
Your presence will be the compass.

If you call me east,
then, God of my father's fathers,
my home is found in Your voice,

and I will go where you lead.

*I will be with you.*

## 123 For You, The Ocean
Long Beach, California

Hey Dad,

I went to the ocean today—
You always loved this place—
but the waves wouldn't wash my tears away.

For a while I closed my eyes,
laid in the sand, and imagined
you were napping next to me,
like that one time in Galveston.
It's much nicer here in Long Beach,
but I'd prefer it be there and then.

I was feeling sad
and I laid silent for a while.
The waves kept crashing in—and I
remembered how much you loved that sound,
so I just listened.

Then, I began to miss the sound of your voice.
So I grabbed my old phone out of my backpack
and listened to the voicemails you left me.

I hope you knew that
you were so important to me—
every time you called and I thought I was busy.

Dad, now it's time for me to hit the road.
Don't worry, Pops,
I'll take you with me everywhere I go.

I love you immensely.
I always have. I always will.
I will continue to miss you
until your voicemails become real.

## 126 Feather
The Colony, Texas

I set out long ago on this ancient road to pre-
pare a place for you to call home. I looked for
sticks that would bend and stretch with need.
I found no such sticks, but I found a base of
ruffled tweed.

I collected my tweed and set out again, undis-
couraged. Then, I looked for wildflowers, but
the wildflower fields were all deserted. In place
of flowers, I found weeds nearby. They weren't
the most beautiful, but still, they seemed
alright.

I took those weeds, and my base of tweed,
and I set out once more, to find the other
things. I thought that diamonds or something
shiny like rubies could do, to decorate this
attempt of a home for you.

Yet, in all my flying, I could never find them.
Instead, I found hard rocks. I settled for rocks
in place of gems.

Much to my dissatisfaction, but little to my
surprise, I found that the home I made was not
pleasant to the eyes.

The time came when there was no more time.
You would soon arrive.

As you came close, I hung my head in shame.
"I'm sorry I couldn't do better," I began, "I'm
really all to blame."

I expected you to disapprove and fly off,
But you lifted my head, looked me in the eyes,

and all my words were lost.

It was then I could see.

While I was busy striving, you too had been
working. I became still as it hit me—
you had brought everything else we could need.

Your sticks were the perfect support to my base
of tweed. You unpacked wildflowers where the
weeds used to be.

To complete our home, you brought out dia-
monds, rubies, and all other sorts of gems.
Then smiling, you asked me to help you
arrange them.

With delight you began to settle into the nest
we prepared together.

And when I asked you how you always seemed
to make my messes beautiful,
you simply responded:

*We will always build home together.*

*I am in the beauty and mess alike.*
*We are two birds of a feather.*

## 127 Home
Sophia, NC

We're not there yet.
We've still got a long, long way to go.

But I know we'll make it—because we've made it.

*Welcome home.*

## ∞ The Fire of Life

There is a flicker,
a sacred torch of life
handed down through the generations.
　　　My father gave me light.

　　　Then his went out.
　　　I was there. I watched it happen.
　　　And my own flame
　　　erupted.

　　　As he took his last breath,
　　　fire ceasing,
his oak closet rod
snapped in two. Some curse was broken.
His coats all fell to the floor.

　　　There's no suffering anymore.

You don't have to believe in the supernatural.
But I watched it happen.
It was sacred. It was holy.
It was unbearably heartbreaking.
And like the coats, I too laid limp.

My spirit knew so much more of what
was happening than my mind ever will.

　　　I sat silent
　　　in a room of smoke.
　　　There were just four of us there beside
　　　him. Silent.
　　　Jesus was there too.
　　　He was not silent.

They are right
when they say grief comes in waves.
But in that moment, I was dropped hundreds

of feet below the surface.
It took a while to breathe normal again.

> I held his hand for a few more minutes
> and pressed my head to his chest.
> Silent.

If you don't know life is fleeting, it is.
And if I can give you anything,
let me give you this:

The raging, brilliant fire of life.
You won't always have it.
But right now, you are burning.

# Acknowledgments

These pages exist because of the support of a faithful few. I would like to express my deepest gratitude to those responsible for helping me create this book.

Blake Steen, thank you for your steady flow of ideas, paired with your careful passion and devotion in editing this work—you are a refreshing river of inspiration. Charlotte Pell and Valina Yen, thank you for crafting a beautiful and meaningful book cover.

To my dad, mom, and the host of extraordinary coaches, teachers, and professors I've had over the years, thank you for offering your wisdom, guidance, and encouragement. In many ways, you nurtured my love for writing with the faithful watering of your time and care.

To the friends and the 144 backers that supported *State Lines* through the Kickstarter campaign—from the bottom of my heart, thank you for your faith and contribution.

Lastly, to the most wholehearted and creative community that I know—quietly tucked away in the woods of North Carolina, loudly awakening the earth to beauty—thank you for helping me discover the way home.

— PH